PICTURING SCOTLAND

ABERDEENSHIRE

NESS PUBLISHING

2   A scene that typifies Aberdeenshire's agricultural hinterland, between Huntly and Turriff.

ABERDEENSHIRE

Introduction: welcome to Aberdeenshire!

If we lived in a world in which the place where you were born was the place you lived all your life and travel to other parts was not the done thing, the people of Aberdeenshire would not have much to complain about. For this mini-world in the north-east of Scotland provides all that is needed to nourish body and soul in an environment that contains as much geographic variety as any reasonable person could wish for. The county has its share of the Cairngorm mountains with a claim to four of the country's nine 4,000ft peaks; a world-famous salmon fishing river; fertile farmland that produces top-quality livestock such as Aberdeen Angus cattle and a wide variety of crops; while its North Sea fishing ports remain at the forefront of this industry despite the challenges that continue to confront it. It is a land rich with ancient monuments, some of which go back to the Neolithic era, and it is home to industries that seek to lead the way in energy technologies to help safeguard the future.

The aim of this book is to take a photographic tour around Aberdeenshire in order to explore its scenic delights, reveal its historic past and simply enjoy the variety of landscape it offers. We start along the northern coast and work southwards in a series of roughly west-to-east and east-to-west strips across the county, eventually reaching what used to be the county of Kincardineshire, now the southernmost district of Aberdeenshire. Therefore we begin at Sandend (opposite), just inside Aberdeenshire's border with neighbouring Moray, on the north coast. Next comes Portsoy, one of

4

As the name suggests, Sandend has a fine beach as well as being a pretty fishing village.   5
This view catches the afterglow on a winter evening.

the earliest fishing villages to be established, with the first harbour being built around 1550, the year it became a burgh. These days, one of Portsoy's main claims to fame is its annual Traditional Boat Festival, held in late June or early July. There are so many photogenic harbours in the county that it has been something of a challenge to photograph them in a variety of ways to avoid a surfeit of similar images.

Many of the county's inland towns are steeped in history and full of architectural interest. Huntly, for example (opposite), is home to a fine castle with 14th-century origins, the Gordon School and the Brander Museum. And on the subject of castles, Aberdeenshire has an amazing number of these, including several of Scotland's most magnificent examples. For every one pictured in this book there are another three or four to be discovered. Stately homes and wonderful gardens are also plentiful. For those who believe finding a great beach means travelling overseas, prepare to

Vessels on display at the Scottish Traditional Boat Festival, Portsoy.

be surprised at what Aberdeenshire has to offer.

This is a big county: Aberdeenshire is the fourth largest council area in Scotland, covering 2439 square miles/6317 square kilometres and the 6th most populous. Its size means that a small book like this cannot do justice to the whole county. Therefore Deeside, all the way from the Cairngorms to the coast at Aberdeen, is the subject of another book in this series; between them these two volumes cover the whole of the county, while a third book concentrates on the city of Aberdeen which forms a separate administrative district.

So now, whether you are a visitor or a resident, let this journey-in-pictures remind you of, or prepare you for, the best that this impressive county has to show. Whether your interest lies in trekking up mountains like Cairn Toul or hills like Bennachie, soaking up the splendour of castles such as Fyvie or Tolquhon, delving into the distant past or roaming endless tracts of unspoilt countryside, let the exploration begin!

Architectural detail in the town of Huntly.   7

8 A panoramic view of the mouth of the River Deveron and the town of Banff. The town goes back to the 12th century, established as a port that traded as part of the important Hanseatic League.

It went on to become a Royal Burgh, receiving its Charter from Robert II in 1372. It was also the county town of Banffshire.

10 Portsoy. The Old (inner) Harbour pictured here is largely that which was built in 1692 by Sir Patrick Ogilvie, the 8th Laird of Boyne, to replace the original one.

This view shows the layout of the old and new harbours, taken during the Scottish Traditional Boat 11
Festival, held at Portsoy. The New Harbour was built to meet the demands of the herring boom.

12 Moving east to Banff, this fine 18th-century John Adam mansion occupies the site of the former Banff Castle and is still generally known by that name. A few fragments of the castle remain.

Duff House, Banff, was designed by William Adam and built from 1735 to 1740 as the seat of the **13** Earls of Fife. It serves as part of the National Galleries of Scotland, housing a range of art treasures.

14 Left: in the historic heart of Banff on Low Street, are the drinking fountain, Mercat Cross, Townhouse and the 1764-built steeple. Right: figures at the top of the Mercat Cross.

On High Shore, a fine array of architecture, with a 17th-century merchant's house on the left. **15**

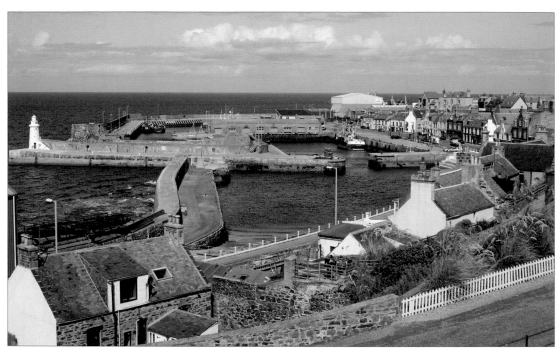

16 Just across the Deveron on the east side of the river is Macduff. When Banff's harbour silted up in the 1800s, Macduff took over as principal port for the area.

Until 1783, Macduff was known as Doune and the Parish Church seen here is still sometimes referred to by this name. Next to it is the town cross and an old anchor that makes an attractive feature.

18 Macduff remains a fishing port and is also active in boat repair. This fishing boat is out of the water for a repaint and maintenance.

Macduff has an excellent Aquarium. This Wolf Fish seems to be giving visitors a cheery welcome. **19**

20 A string of fishing villages was built in the coves along the northern coast, such as this one at Gardenstown in Gamrie Bay; a charming village with narrow streets and tightly packed cottages.

In the next bay east lies delightful Pennan, famous as the location for the film Local Hero. **21**
The village has suffered greatly from coastal erosion in the form of cliff mudslides.

22 Further along the coast is Rosehearty, which was probably established by Danish fishermen as long ago as the 14th century. Boats out of water add a different aspect to the scene.

Left: This sculpture in Fraserburgh underlines that it is one of Aberdeenshire's major fishing ports. **23**
Right: This ornate 19th-century drinking fountain is at Saltoun Place in Fraserburgh.

24 Taken from just outside Rosehearty, this view looks across Aberdour Bay and Cullykhan Bay, with Troup Head in the distance on the right – a scene that typifies the rugged Aberdeenshire coastline.

26 A line-up of five trawlers in Fraserburgh harbour. The fish market covers 2,092 square metres and can handle 6,000 boxes daily. The port lands about 40,000 tons of fish annually.

Kinnaird Head Lighthouse, Fraserburgh (Historic Scotland). A guided tour of this lighthouse is the **27** highlight of a visit to the Museum of Scottish Lighthouses, located close by.

28 We now follow an inland course across the county from west to east, starting at Huntly in Strath Bogie, where this magnificent carpet of crocuses lights up the approach to the Gordon School.

Retailers in Huntly have set up a Rewards Loyalty Card scheme designed to encourage local **29** shopping and stave off the impact of supermarkets. This shop is a member of the scheme.

30 Huntly Castle, main seat of the Gordons, served as a baronial residence for five centuries. Many impressive features include fine heraldic sculpture and inscribed stone friezes (Historic Scotland).

The remains of the castle courtyard viewed from the old motte. On the left of the picture is the site **31** of the Tower House, built around 1410 and blown up in 1594 in an attack by King James VI.

32 GlenDronach Distillery, near the village of Forgue. Founded in 1826, it has had several owners, but in 2008 a renaissance began: the BenRiach Distillery Company became GlenDronach's proud new owner.

Turriff town centre, looking down the High Street. The town's origins date back to a Columban **33** monastery built nearby in around 1000AD. Turriff is north-east of Huntly, linked by the River Deveron.

34 The Haughs during Turriff Agricultural Show. This is the largest annual event to be held in Aberdeenshire and is the largest two-day Show in Scotland.

Continuing eastwards across the county, not far from the village of Maud, **35** we come to Deer Abbey, the remains of a Cistercian monastery founded in 1219.

36 A short distance on is Aden Country Park, in which the Aberdeenshire Farming Museum is located. Many exhibits are housed in this unique, semi-circular Home Farm steading.

Hareshowe Farmhouse has been moved from its original site some miles away and rebuilt at the **37** Farming Museum complete with its cottage garden. The farmhouse is open to visitors.

38 The Loch of Strathbeg nature reserve, Britain's largest dune loch, is a joy to visit at any time of year. In winter, thousands of wild geese (especially pink-footed geese), swans and ducks fly in.

Peterhead is the UK's leading white-fish port and one of the largest in Europe. During 2010 **39** landings of all types of fish amounted to 170,000 tonnes. Inset: fishwife and child statue, Peterhead.

40 We now reach the east coast of Aberdeenshire and look down on Peterhead's great harbour.
The port comprises two areas – Peterhead Bay Harbour and the Harbours of Peterhead.

Today the port deals with a variety of cargoes and is also involved in the North Sea oil and gas industry.   41
The town has a population of over 17,500.

42 For the adventurous, coastal rock climbing can be enjoyed at many places. In this view, the ruins of Slains Castle (near Cruden Bay) can be seen in the background (© Aberdeen City and Shire Regional Identity).

The unspoilt sands of Cruden Bay, a seaside holiday village which once boasted its own **43** tramway that connected the railway station to the Cruden Bay Hotel. See also p.77.

44 Turning west and inland now, the town of Ellon is attractively set on the banks of the river Ythan. Inset: a modern sculpture of an otter stands at the Bridge Street roundabout.

A few miles west of Ellon is the superb Pitmedden Garden. The formal walled garden was originally **45** laid out in 1675 by Sir Alexander Seton and recreated in the 1950s by the National Trust for Scotland.

46 Aberdeenshire is graced by many historic castles, but Tolquhon is one of the most picturesque. The oldest part is the stump of an early 15th-century tower house (Historic Scotland).

Continuing west from Tolquhon Castle we reach the hilltop town of Old Meldrum, just outside **47** which is the Lochter Activity Centre. Fishing features alongside more vigorous activities.

48 Not far from Old Meldrum, the historic little village and Parish of Tarves lies in the heart of the Aberdeenshire countryside. This is its Heritage Centre, complete with vintage petrol pump.

A few miles west of Ellon is the superb Pitmedden Garden. The formal walled garden was originally **45** laid out in 1675 by Sir Alexander Seton and recreated in the 1950s by the National Trust for Scotland.

46 Aberdeenshire is graced by many historic castles, but Tolquhon is one of the most picturesque. The oldest part is the stump of an early 15th-century tower house (Historic Scotland).

Continuing west from Tolquhon Castle we reach the hilltop town of Old Meldrum, just outside **47** which is the Lochter Activity Centre. Fishing features alongside more vigorous activities.

48 Not far from Old Meldrum, the historic little village and Parish of Tarves lies in the heart of the Aberdeenshire countryside. This is its Heritage Centre, complete with vintage petrol pump.

From Tarves, it's a short step north to Haddo House. This spectacular country house was designed **49** by William Adam and built from 1732 to 1736 (National Trust for Scotland).

50 Just a mile from Haddo is the village of Methlick, with its particularly attractive garden of remembrance around the war memorial. The old churchyard lies beyond.

Aberdeenshire boasts many Neolithic sites such as Loanhead of Daviot recumbent stone circle **51** (south of Fyvie). It was constructed between 4,000 and 5,000 years ago.

52 Fyvie Castle is near the village of the same name, north of Old Meldrum.
This ornamental loch lies in the extensive parklands that surround the castle.

The castle itself is a truly magnificent structure, the origins of which go back to the 13th century. **53**
The opulent Edwardian interiors (National Trust for Scotland) are a joy to behold.

54 Bennachie dominates central Aberdeenshire. It has three peaks of which Mither Tap, above, at the eastern end of the ridge is the most prominent. This is the view from the north.

This is the granite outcrop of Mither Tap seen in close-up. The remains of an ancient hill fort are still **55** prominent on the far side of the outcrop. The walk up here is relatively easy and very rewarding.

56 Aberdeenshire is excellent cattle farming country. This panorama taken near the village of Hillhead of Durno (west of Loanhead) shows the three tops of Bennachie in the distance.

Bennachie ('Sacred Hill') is a possible location for the battle of Mons Graupius, in which the Romans defeated the Caledonians.

58 The view north from Oxencraig, highest of the Bennachie summits and seen towards the right in the previous picture, surveys the agricultural plains stretching away as far as the eye can see.

So far we have criss-crossed northern Aberdeenshire to this central point. Next we venture **59** westwards, in due course reaching Strath Don, the area seen here from the top of Mither Tap.

60 North-west of Bennachie is Dunideer hill fort. The remains of a 13th-century castle can be seen atop the hill, but settlement on this site probably goes back to the Iron Age (see also back cover).

Dunideer gives grandstand views in all directions. Looking west, in this pastoral patchwork, harvest is **61** well advanced in the arable fields. The Inverness–Aberdeen railway can be seen in the centre.

62 To the east of Dunideer, we have a panoramic view of the town of Insch.
Some remains of the ancient hilltop settlement can be seen in the foreground.

One of Insch's more interesting features is St Drostan's Old Kirkyard. St Drostan, one of **63** St Columba's twelve companions, brought Christianity to Insch in the late 6th century.

64 Left: in a field just outside Insch stands the Picardy Stone, a carved, Pictish monolith set within an earlier (no longer visible) burial cairn. Right: the 9th-century Pictish Maiden Stone stands near Oyne.

West of Insch at Kennethmont is Leith Hall Garden & Estate. A huge variety of flowering trees, **65** shrubs, roses, fruit and vegetables provide interest all year round (National Trust for Scotland).

66 En route to Strath Don we pass through Rhynie with its pleasing village square and Noth Parish Church beyond. The hill in the distance is Tap o' Noth, still snow-pocketed in late April.

Southwards now to Donside: even in its ruined state Kildrummy Castle stands serene and confident. **67**
Also not to be missed is Glenbuchat Castle, a few miles west (both Historic Scotland).

68 Next to the castle is Donside's best-kept secret – Kildrummy Castle Gardens. An extensive walk passes through water gardens, woodland and the Quarry Garden, seen here.

South of Kildrummy, a particularly lovely valley runs down to the village of Towie. **69**
The landscape seen here captures the rural essence of Aberdeenshire particularly well.

70 Continuing westwards reveals the wonderful scenery of upper Strath Don. This vista looks north towards Corgarff, Cockbridge and the hills of the Lecht.

Corgarff Castle stands in splendid yet strategic isolation in upper Strath Don. Dating back to the 15th century, this fine tower house has had an inevitably turbulent history (Historic Scotland).

72 Rural Donside between Kildrummy and Glenkindie, seen during harvest-time at dawn. The hill in the distance on the left is Morven, 872m/2860ft.

74 Near the Lecht Ski Centre, the deep snows of winter enfold the hills above Strath Don. The outcropping tors on the skyline are typical of this part of the Cairngorms.

We now return eastwards down the valley of the River Don to the town of Alford. **75**
The Alford Valley 2ft narrow-gauge railway runs from the former BR station to Haughton Park.

76 Alford Heritage Centre is an Aladdin's Cave of artefacts, implements and every sort of item from the past, including this reconstruction of a village shop from yesteryear.

The excellent Grampian Transport Museum completes Alford's line-up of attractions. **77**
The tram pictured here used to operate on the Cruden Bay tramway (see p.43).

78 Continuing down the Don we arrive at the delightful village of Monymusk. The houses around The Square were originally built between 1728 and 1732, and rebuilt in the 1890s.

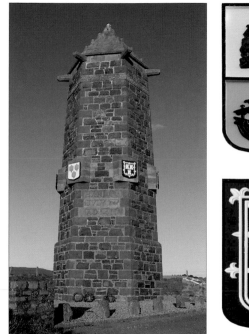

Memorial to the Battle of Harlaw which took place near Inverurie in July 1411. To mark the battle's 600th anniversary in 2011, the crests of some of the protagonists were added to the monument. **79**

80 The Great North of Scotland Railway was established in the mid 1840s and had its engineering work-shops at Inverurie. It built some fine stations, as this picture of Inverurie station waiting room shows.

Inverurie is where the River Urie flows into the Don. The town's pleasing Market Place has **81** the War Memorial as its centrepiece, with the 1863-built Town Hall beyond.

82 Not far south of Inverurie is Castle Fraser, one of the grandest Castles of Mar. Completed in 1636, it contains an evocative Great Hall, fine furniture and works of art (National Trust for Scotland).

Left: Rooftop detail as seen from one of Castle Fraser's turrets. **83**
Right: Looking into the Castle Gardens from the same vantage point.

84 Also close to Inverurie is East Aquhorthies recumbent stone circle. 'Recumbent' refers to the stone placed horizontally between two upright stones, as seen here. Bennachie broods in the distance.

Southwards, towards Deeside, is Craigievar. This fairytale castle, a fine example of Scottish Baronial **85** architecture, has recently undergone a thorough restoration (National Trust for Scotland).

86 The view from the castle takes in more typical (stunning!) Aberdeenshire scenery, with heather-clad Benaquhallie rising above a mixed farming landscape.

Continuing south, just by the village of Lumphanan is the Peel Ring. Built by an incoming **87** Norman family, the earthwork used to have a palisade around the top, from which 'peel' is derived.

88 Now for the first time we venture south of Deeside and into the hills between there and the Kincardine coast. The route through these parts is known as the Cairn o' Mount road, in reference

to its summit point. But prior to this it passes by Clachnaben (589m/1932ft), topped by its very prominent granite tor. This is a rewarding and not too strenuous walk that takes about three hours.

90 Before focusing on Aberdeenshire's southern districts, another look at Morven, first seen on p.72, this time viewed from Glen Gairn. It's a Cairngorms mountain that deserves more attention than it gets.

Having crossed Deeside (see Introduction), we arrive at Stonehaven in the former county of Kincardineshire. Here, at the dawn of a beautiful day, the sun is just reaching into the harbour.

92 The classic view of Stonehaven. The harbour is the historic focus of the town, the first breakwater being built in the 1500s. If the sea is too cold, there is a heated, outdoor seawater swimming pool.

On the right is the Tolbooth, the oldest building in Stonehaven, **93** constructed c.1600 by the Earl Marischal.

94 From much more recent times, this superb Art Deco restaurant is one of Stonehaven's must-see sights. The interior provides a wonderfully atmospheric taste of the 1930s.

A typical coastal scene near Dunnottar Castle.

96 Dunnottar Castle, just outside Stonehaven, is one of Scotland's most iconic, not to mention most defensible, perched high on this rocky promontory and almost surrounded by the sea.

The site on which the Castle sits has been inhabited since Pictish times although an exact date is
not known. This view shows Waterton's Lodging on the left and the Keep on the right.

98 About 10 miles down the coast from Stonehaven is the village of Inverbervie, seen here on a bright spring day. Scotland's first water-powered flax mill was built here in 1787.

Hercules Linton, designer of the famous clipper, Cutty Sark, was born in Inverbervie in 1837.

The Cutty Sark was built at Dumbarton in 1869 and is now beautifully preserved at Greenwich.

The memorial, dedicated by the people of Inverbervie on 11 July 1997, replaces a memorial unveiled by Sir Francis Chichester in 1969. It is a full scale replica of the ship's figurehead and was carved from Hercules Linton's original drawings.

The figurehead depicts the comely young witch in Burns' poem Tam o' Shanter grasping the tail of Tam's grey mare.

Linton died in the house where he was born and is buried in Inverbervie Kirkyard.

One of Inverbervie's more notable claims to fame is its connection with the famous sailing ship **99** *Cutty Sark*. Left: this plaque tells the story. Right: the replica of the ship's figurehead.

100 Left: A short distance inland we come to Arbuthnott, home of the Centre devoted to the life and times of Lewis Grassic Gibbon, one of Scotland's best known authors. Right: Also in Arbuthnott, . . .

... the Kirk of St Ternan is one of the few Parish churches in rural Scotland that dates from pre-Reformation times and is still in use for public worship. Above: the stained-glass windows behind the altar.

102 West of Arbuthnott is the picturesque village of Fettercairn. The rich red sandstone buildings are seen to good effect through the Royal Arch, erected in 1864 to celebrate Queen Victoria's visit in 1861.

A harvest-time view of the historic Fettercairn Distillery, founded in 1824, with the Cairngorms
rising in the distance. Tours are available from May to September.

104 Just across the fields from Fettercairn is the small town of Laurencekirk. Situated in the region known as the Howe o' the Mearns, this panoramic view of the town and its surrounding countryside

shows clearly why agriculture has always been one of the main sources of employment.

106 From Laurencekirk, a short hop back from the coast leads to Johnshaven, where charming cottages like this show off traditional features like window shutters and pantile roofs.

As a historic fishing village, it's perhaps not surprising that Johnshaven hosts the annual Fish Festival. Above: moody light at the harbour.

108 The dramatic view from Aberdeenshire's most westerly point, close to the summit of Braeriach (1296m/4252ft) in the Cairngorms, looking east towards Cairn Toul (1291m/4236ft) and into the Larig Ghru.

High above Deeside, this is Lochnagar (1155m/3789ft), the mountain that,
somewhat confusingly, takes its name from the corrie lochan in the picture.

110 One of Lochnagar's neighbouring mountains is Broad Cairn (998m/3274ft), from the summit of which we look down into Loch Muick, the largest loch in the Cairngorms.

And finally the superb vista from the summit of Lochnagar down into Royal Deeside – but that is **111** the subject of another journey and another book . . .

Published 2012 by Ness Publishing, 47 Academy Street, Elgin, Moray, IV30 1LR
Phone/fax 01343 549663 www.nesspublishing.co.uk
(First edition published in 2009 entitled Aberdeenshire: a pictorial souvenir).

All photographs © Colin and Eithne Nutt except p.19 © Macduff Aquarium; p.21 © Lyn Macdonald;
pp.21 & 40/41 © Scotavia Images; p.42 © Aberdeen City and Shire Regional Identity; p.98 © Jim Henderson.

Text © Colin Nutt
ISBN 978-1-906549-34-3

Front cover: Fraserburgh harbour; p.1: ornate street lamps in Banff; p.4: Great North of Scotland Railway crest;
this page: Brandsbutt Pictish symbol stone, Inverurie; back cover: castle ruins at Dunideer hill fort.

For a list of websites and phone numbers please turn over >

Websites and phone numbers (where available) for principal places featured in this book in order of appearance:

Aberdeenshire: www.aberdeencityandshire.com / www.aberdeenshire.gov.uk
Fraserburgh: www.visitfraserburgh.com
Portsoy: www.portsoyhome.co.uk
Scottish Traditional Boat Festival: stbf.bizland.com (T) 01261 842951
Huntly: www.huntly.net
Banff: www.bestofbanffshire.co.uk
Banff Castle: www.banffcastle.org.uk (T) 01261 815325
Duff House: www.duffhouse.org.uk (T) 01261 818181
Macduff: www.banff-macduff.com (T) 01261 812419 (Tourist Information)
Macduff Aquarium: www.macduff-aquarium.org.uk (T) 01261 833369
Pennan: www.aboutaberdeen.com/pennan
Museum of Scottish Lighthouses: www.lighthousemuseum.org.uk (T) 01346 511022
Fraserburgh Heritage Centre: www.fraserburghheritage.com (T) 01346 512888
Huntly Castle: www.historic-scotland.gov.uk (T) 01466 793191
GlenDronach Distillery: www.glendronachdistillery.co.uk (T) 01466 730202
Turriff: www.newturra.co.uk
Turriff Agricultural Show: www.turriffshow.org (T) 01888 568830
Deer Abbey: www.historic-scotland.gov.uk (T) 01667 460232
Aberdeenshire Farming Museum: www.aberdeenshire.gov.uk/museums (T) 01771 624590
Loch of Strathbeg: www.rspb.org.uk (T) 01346 532017
Peterhead: www.peterheadonline.com
Cruden Bay: www.crudenbay.org.uk
Ellon: www.visitellon.co.uk
Pitmedden Garden: www.nts.org.uk (T) 0844 493 2177
Tolquhon Castle: www.historic-scotland.gov.uk (T) 01651 851286
Lochter Activity Centre: www.lochter.co.uk (T) 01651 872000